A Long Goodbye

A Long Goodbye

Poems for Caregivers and Loved Ones
of Those Suffering with Dementia

by Judith Zottoli

ISBN-13: 978-1523363537
ISBN-10: 1523363533

Book design by John Waterman
Published by Judith Zottoli through CreateSpace.com
Printed in the United States of America

CONTENTS

Preface		5
Brain Chatter		7
Wedding	(photo)	8
Words		9
Grief		10
Loss		11
Tears		12
The Anniversary		13
Ed and Flowers	(photo)	14
Flower Comfort		15
Sunset		16
Dementia		17
Planting Zinnias	(photo)	18
Ed's Garden		19
Au Revoir		20
Ed's Lament		21
Lagoon at Biltmore	(photo)	22
Caregiver		23

CarePartners	(photo)	24
Biltmore Gates		25
Bob and Ed	(photo)	26
Dark to Light		27
Friends	(photo)	28
Home		29
Out to Dinner	(photo)	30
Lost		31
Ed and Son	(photo)	32
Embracing the Rose		33
Conversations		34
Veterans Home	(photo)	36
Charles		37
Ed and Cat	(photo)	38
To Ed		39
Beside the Lake	(photo)	40
Forgotten		41
Social Self		42

Special Moments		43
Dearest Ed		44
Ed and Judy	(photo)	45
Acknowledgments		46
About the Author		47

This book is dedicated to my loving husband, Ed.

Preface

In July of 2008, Ed shouted, “Get in the bedroom and don’t come out.” I went in the bedroom and locked the door. This was unusual behavior for him, and was one of the symptoms that led to the diagnosis of vascular dementia and a mild cognitive disorder.

When I met Ed in 1987, he was an owner of a small company called Tally Ho. They made horseback riding products from lambs wool and leather. Prior to this he was a co-owner of a manufacturing firm that made flight simulators. He was in the United States Air Force for four years in the late 1960’s. Ed retired in 1988.

We married in 1993 and rented an apartment in Hingham, Massachusetts. I was a branch librarian at the Thomas Crane Public Library in Quincy. We had a lot in common and loved to dance, hike, canoe, listen to jazz and travel. Ed was, and is, a very social person. He met people easily and was good natured.

When I think back, in the early years of our marriage, he was showing signs of dementia. Unbeknownst to me, he was in debt and went through bankruptcy. He listened to tapes on the power of positive thinking while I was at work. He read books on how to make a million and took a course on speed reading. He said he was depressed and went to see a psychologist.

In 2003 we moved to Brunswick, Maine. I was a part-time reference librarian at two local libraries and Ed worked part-time in sales. He did not keep his job for long as his memory was bad. In the five years we lived there, I noticed symptoms that did not seem normal. In 2008, Ed saw a neurologist who said he had personality aberration, deviation from normal, and suggested he should get a geriatric assessment at Maine Medical Center in Portland. We went there and Ed had cognitive testing. They said he did not meet the criteria for dementia and we should go for couples' counseling. I cried all the way home.

In April of 2009 we moved to Asheville, North Carolina, chased by the snow and cold of Maine. We found a primary care physician who diagnosed dementia and recommended we make an appointment with MemoryCare. The physician at MemoryCare diagnosed cognitive impairment due to a progressive neurodegenerative condition that caused early stage dementia.

For the next six years, Ed got progressively worse, although we still shared the love of my three biological children and he continued to let me shine within by supporting and encouraging my writing. Thanks to my support groups, MemoryCare, Dr. Battle, CarePartners Adult Day Care, the Veterans Administration, and the Greenwood Inn, I was able to keep Ed at home.

On September 12, 2014, one of the hardest days of my life, I took Ed to the North Carolina State Veterans Nursing Home in Black Mountain, North Carolina. I could no longer take care of him at home. My feelings and emotions are expressed in my poems. I hope other caregivers of those who suffer from this terrible disease can relate to my poems.

Brain Chatter

I walk through woods
so deep,
I might drown in them.

Brain chatter shuts out
beauty,
inside, outside my head.

After the enactment
of he said, she said,
passes,

I fill my cup with
the echo of the wood thrush,
a layer of pine needles,
the soft smell of balsam,
verdant, lacy fern.

As I leave the forest,
I feel
the warmth of the sun
on my face.

Judith Zottoli (May 2008)

Wedding, 1993

Words

Words clutter his mind,
slip and slide
in and out.

Words in his head
spin around,
do not birth.

Thoughts minus cognition
tumble out
without recognition.

Memory fades,
sun sets,
night falls.

Judith Zottoli (December 2009)

Grief

Who will I meet today,
dear husband,
Dr. Jekyll or Mr. Hyde
in this dance of reason.

I grieve that which is gone
through anger, tears, love.
Who is this man,
I once knew,
teenager who resents
his parent
shows no appreciation
for the caregiver
I have become.

Judith Zottoli (February 2010)

Loss

One minute
he is my
gentle giant
with a mind
of four,
an intelligent adult
the next.

I become angry
with the innocent child
until I remember
I am dealing
with dementia.

The agony
of our loss
creates hollows
deep within
the weeping willow
whose branches shed
the tears
of my soul.

Judith Zottoli (March 2010)

Tears

I cried when he had no memory of yesterday.

I cried when he no longer understood me.

I cried when he went to MemoryCare.

I cried when his golf partners shunned him,

and then I cried for me,

a keening that came from a deep place,

washing away my grief,

for a while.

Judith Zottoli (June 2010)

The Anniversary

I want a husband not a child.

I want to be understood, not forgotten.

I'm tired of, "He can't help it."

He looks like the handsome, intelligent man

I married eighteen years ago.

Judith Zottoli (July 2010)

Ed with Flowers (December 2011)

Flower Comfort

The fog of his mind
lifts above
the silent flowers
at Biltmore Gardens
bringing peace.

We enter the greenhouse.
The scent of asiatic lillies
fills the air with the
fragrant, soft perfume of
flamingo fire, palms and ivy.

A baroque violin concerto
feels playful and happy.
We waltz
to the music
in each others arms.

Exhausted, we sit
on iron garden seats
in meditation,
taking in the beauty
of the moment.

Judith Zottoli (December 2011)

Sunset

Sunrise, sunset,
one by one,
gone.

I am losing you
to another realm.
Memories we shared,
intimacy we knew,

one by one,
gone.

Judith Zottoli (January 2011)

Dementia

I feel the weight
of my grief
as his mind
sinks
in
quicksand.

Sometimes …

he feels the weight
of his grief
as his mind
sinks
in
quicksand .

Judith Zottoli (March 2013)

Planting Zinnias (July 2013)

Ed's Garden

Last year,
Ed seeded Zinnias
in a greenhouse.
He planted outside
in May.

Red , yellow, purple blossoms
resplendent with butterflies
beautified our lives.

This year, Zinnias
spring from garden to garden,
lawn to cement cracks,
Ed's hunger for life strong
in the energy of his blooms.

Judith Zottoli (August 2013)

Au Revoir

For now dear Ed,

Adieu
in-depth talks,

Adieu
traveling,

Adieu
driving your car,

Adieu
your finances,

Adieu
independence.

Dance on my love.
Dixieland lives,

Au revoir...

Judith Zottoli (July 2013)

Ed's Lament

I'm losing everything. I can't
fight the fog.
I am frightened
of becoming
your child.

I don't remember
anything about this.
What's happening
to me?

I need to get a job. Do we
have enough money?
Something is wrong with me.
I have to work on it.

I dreamed I stored all
my things in boxes.
When I woke up,
they were gone.

Judith Zottoli (March 2013)

Lagoon at Biltmore (2013)

Caregiver

Sometimes I feel like a husbandless wife.
Let my grief be gone.

I feel solitary.
Let my grief be gone.

I am isolated.
Let my grief be gone.

I hear the death of his mind.
Let my grief be gone.

Sometimes I feel like a husbandless wife.
Let my grief be gone.

Judith Zottoli November 2013)

CarePartners Adult Day Care (2013)

Biltmore Gates

We enter the Biltmore Gates
and he says
I have never been here before.

I could have said
you have been here
hundreds of times.

Each visit
he sees the beauty
for the first time.

Long rolling fields
edged with sunflowers,
glass lagoon reflects
shades of green and gold.
Rose aroma creates
pleasant euphoria.

We exit Biltmore Gates.
I feel sad.
He will forget this morning.

I will remember
his pleasure
and our loss.

Judith Zottoli (August 2014)

Bob and Ed (2014)

Dark to Light

The sun fades.
Night dims to darkness.
Words don't express
the sadness I feel.

In despair,
I put my love
in a nursing home,
to calm his confusion.

I say to him:
You are in my heart.
I am in yours.
This is our home.

He smiles. I repeat:
You are in my heart.
I am in yours.
This is our home.

He smiles again.
I have hope,
as the moon rises
and darkness fades.

Judith Zottoli (November 2014)

Friends (2014)

Home

Just when I thought
nothing could get worse,
the clouds descended
on me, wet with grief.

He asked me
where we came from.
I told him Maine.
He asked me
where is that?
I do not know
where I am.
I told him
not to worry.
We will stay.
You are safe.
We are home.

The sun came out.
He said to me,
you are beautiful.
and I love you.

Judith Zottoli (June 2014)

Out to Dinner (2014)

Lost

I am lost. You save
me from being in
total confusion. It
makes me feel like somebody
when I see you. When
I eat I know what
to do and what to ask.

Without you I run
around trying to find
out what to do. I know
less and less. I have
to work so hard not
to forget you. The
people here are changing
in my eyes, all the time.

Sometimes I can't find you.
Now you are here. I need
another hug. I love you.

Judith Zottoli (December 2014)

Ed and Son (2014)

Embracing the Rose

When the rose blooms
I savor the soft, red petals,
the aroma fills my senses
and yet when I touch it
I feel the thorns.

My heart weeps guilt that
I am here in our home
eating at our table
sitting in the recliner on the porch
with the cat nestled in my lap.

I go to see my husband
in his new home
where his mental
and physical needs
are met by others.

I love him, laugh with him
in the happiness of the moment.
I walk out the door alone, in despair,
but still embrace the rose,
not the thorns.

Judith Zottoli (April 2015)

Conversations

Everyone is covered
with sparkling fairydust
in this never never land,
the nursing home where
my husband lives. Every
meal he sits at the table
with his three friends
James, William and Henry.
They sit in silence,
the table covered in
a white-linen tablecloth.

This morning I arrive at
breakfast. I watch them
relate to each other with
familiarity and contentment.
I say good morning. James
high fives me, William says
he has to go to work and
Henry nods his head.
Ed jumps up and hugs me.
Ed and I leave the table
to go to his room.

Ed goes back to his friends
to tell them in a whisper
that we are going in the bedroom.
They smile, their eyes twinkle.
In the bedroom Ed tells me
someone is sleeping in his
bed. He must lie in it to
keep them out.

The nurse tells me this is
true. His friend James
thinks Ed's room is his and
wanders in to take a nap.

There is friendship and
caring, silence and softness
between these children of God.

Judith Zottoli (February 2015)

NC State Veterans Home, Black Mountain (2015)

Charles

Charles is an angel.
Ed's friend of 75 years
visits him every month
in the nursing home.

Long distances,
busy lives,
denial and fear
keep family and friends away,
and create isolation
for Ed and me.

Charles is an angel
who never gives up
on his friend
who is disappearing.

Judith Zottoli (June 2015)

Ed and Cat (2015)

To Ed

I ask a favor you can't grant, old friend,
as you and I and Giles approach the end:
Remember Kenilworth and Brunswick Streets-
The vacant lot above your house, a place
for hideouts, forts and even baseball games.
(your mother, nervous, glancing out, retreats,
her windows safe.) Recall the constant chase:
the Aherns' Laddie, my Patcheye, all names
that pale against your poodle, Pierrot.
And then the teenage summers, Morewood Lake-
the tiles we dove for, streams explored by boat.
The Indianhead and Showboat, Newt and Jake.
For you, Ed, Gil and I will hold this trove
of what – we never would admit – was love.

Charles Reynolds (August 2015)

Beside the Lake (2014)

Forgotten

My deepest fear is
that Ed will forget who I am.
When I leave the nursing home I wonder
will he remember me next time.

So far, he hesitates,
places me in his mind and
a smile lights up his face.

Our son walked into his room.
Ed did not know him.
The sadness on Mark's face
tore at my heart.

The thought that
I may be next to disappear
from his memory
haunts me.

Judith Zottoli Aurust 2015)

Social Self

I telephone my sister:
"Hi, how are you?" says Ruth.
"I'm great," says Ed.

He fools so many.
Others do not hear
the word confusion,
or memory loss.
They think he is fine.

The reality:
Lost identity while
social skills persist.
As the storm rages on
he is lost at sea.

I rain tears
for all we have loved
and lost.

Judith Zottoli (August 2015)

Special Moments

God has brushed me
with a new kind of love.

Ed says to me:
You are prettier
than those flowers.
You are my sweetie.
I love you.
Give me a hug.

Judith Zottoli (August 2015)

Dearest Ed

This I know for sure.
I will always love
who you were, and
who you have become
in this life and beyond.

The sun will rise,
The sun will set.
Tomorrow will come
and God is in His House.

Love, Judsie

Judith Zottoli August 2015)

Ed and Judy, 1988

Acknowledgments

I want to thank Dr. Battle; MemoryCare and Mary and Pat, the leaders of the support groups; CarePartners Adult Day Care; the Veterans Administration; Greenwood Inn; and the North Carolina State Veterans Nursing Home, Black Mountain, in particular Georgia of Ward D, and all the kind people who work there. Thanks to Ray Russell and the Asheville Writers Group for all their critical suggestions. Thanks to John Waterman for his help in publishing this book.

About the Author

Judith Zottoli was born in Boston, lived in Maine and Newfoundland where her three children grew up. She attended the University of Maine and Simmons College where she earned a library degree. Her poetry appears in *Memories: a collection of poems* and *Blue Bus to Serre: A Memoir.* She lives in Asheville, North Carolina. Her husband, Edward Floyd, the inspiration for this book, passed away on September 4, 2015.

Notes

77032251R00031

Made in the USA
Lexington, KY
22 December 2017